Kathryn's visionary verse of landscapes temporal and spiritual invokes a presence deeply needed in Mormon culture—the eminent absent Mother. She reveals the sacred feminine as spiritual survival. In feminist eco-fashion she sees invisible connections between animate and inanimate, the miraculous within mundane.

She accepts the challenge of Mormon theology, to translate spirit from materia, as living soul. Her images are aflame, impossible to ignore, arresting attention to awakening the self, body and soul. In the gaps between our molecules she sees electrons marry form and energy, architecture and theology. She finds "the axis of absolute reality" in every moment, by walking an inner landscape to the "cosmic odeum" in the center of our own being. Her facile grasp of poetic technique woos truth from words. Read at your own risk: you will be consumed by the alchemy catalyzed within these pages.

–Maxine Hanks
editor of *Women and Authority:*
Re-emerging Mormon Feminism

The Tree at the Center is a beautiful debut volume of poetry that is intelligent and sincere in its look at our wilderness mother, indeed our Heavenly Mother, and the language of women. This book breaks through silence and is also full of an honest look at the speaker's own experience with motherhood. The poems speak about *a voice, at this / distant opening in the sky / not of humankind, not of beast or rain, / that breaks my heart / open as Rilke's birds do* ("Horizon"). In that rich language and voice found here we get to experience something both new and familiar and dear. Something that stirs and is wild. In Kathryn's words: *There / is the Mother, on bended knee / in the great mind of the body, / spurring the horses on / and on and on* ("Labor").

–Laura Stott
author of *In the Museum of Coming and Going*

Sonntag's remarkable debut collection is an ode to God the Mother, "Her thousand ears, / Her thousand eyes," a deft weaving of scripture, temple symbology, ecological awareness, and lyricism. The poet rewinds creation's narrative, repositioning the Mother as the Tree at the Center, the womb, the "urtext of women," pregnant fullness and postpartum empty. She knows grief's wolf, yet remains rooted to earth and spans the heavens, "Her thousand branches adorning the long climb / into the milky stars[.]" This book is a welcome and timely contribution to the ongoing, critical work of uncovering the Mother.

—Dayna Patterson
co-editor of *Dove Song: Heavenly Mother in Mormon Poetry*

THE TREE AT
THE CENTER

BY COMMON CONSENT PRESS is a non-profit publisher dedicated to producing affordable, high-quality books that help define and shape the Latter-day Saint experience. BCC Press publishes books that address all aspects of Mormon life. Our mission includes finding manuscripts that will contribute to the lives of thoughtful Latter-day Saints, mentoring authors and nurturing projects to completion, and distributing important books to the Mormon audience at the lowest possible cost.

THE TREE AT THE CENTER

Kathryn Knight Sonntag

The Tree at the Center
Copyright © 2019 by Kathryn Knight Sonntag

All rights reserved. Printed in the United States of America. No part of this book may be used or reproduced in any manner whatsoever without written permission except in the case of brief quotations embodied in critical articles or reviews.

For information contact
By Common Consent Press
4062 S. Evelyn Dr.
Salt Lake City, UT 84124-2250

Book design: Andrew Heiss

Cover design: Mikey Brooks

Cover image: *Stylized tree flanked by ibexes, 9th-8th century BCE*

Excavations begun in the 1970s at ʻAjrud, an archaeological site on the Sinai Peninsula in present-day Egypt, revealed two large pithos jars with intriguing drawings and text. The line drawing on the cover depicts the Tree of Life, representing the goddess Asherah. Two ibexes flank the tree and eat from its leaves. The textual inscriptions found on the jars are, mostly, written in early Hebrew script. They frequently mention Yahweh.

www.bccpress.org

ISBN-10: 1-948218-16-X
ISBN-13: 978-1-948218-16-0

10 9 8 7 6 5 4 3 2 1

For my first child Rainer,
and my second inside me.

For all who seek the Divine Feminine.

CONTENTS

Introduction ix

I. The Tree of Ascent 1

Nüshu 5
Horizon 6
The Center 8
Fallacy of a Distant Sky God 10
The Tree of Life 11
World Tree 12
The Call 14
Holy of Holies 15

II. The Tree of Fertility 17

Salvation Pantoum 21
From Eve's Imperative Guide on How to
   Tend and Till the Earth Our Mother:
     How To Conduct a Prescribed Burn in Grassland 22
Full Circle 24
Reprise 25
The Ever Existent Image 26
Baba Yaga 28
Woman of Willendorf 30
Treasures in Heaven 32
Labor 33
"Plate 18," by Unknown 35
As a Mother 38

	Nine Months Postpartum	40
	Postpartum Depression	42
	Woman Like a Wolf	44
	Palimpsest	45
	Miscarriage	47
	Creation	48
	Renascence	49
	III. Asherah the Tree	51
	One Thousand Two Hundred Sixty Days	55
	The Tree at the Center	56
	Particle Mother	58
	The Older Covenant	60
	Cube of Fire	62
	The Mercy Seat	63
	Ezekiel's Visions	64
	She Who Joins Together	66
	Wo, Wo is Me, the Mother of Men	67
	Salvation	68
	In One	69
	The Grove	70
Acknowledgments		73
Notes		75

INTRODUCTION

As a landscape designer who works on Latter-day Saint temple landscapes, I am often left wondering where the symbol of the Mother—if not in the garden and not in the Holy of Holies—has place to reside. Latter-day Saint women around the world grapple with these urgent questions: Where is a divine feminine figure located in LDS theology? Where does She lodge here on Earth? And because there isn't a prescribed answer, every woman must find Her for herself. This is my answer to my questions, a journey into the wilderness that has lead me to an ever-evolving image of what it is to return to the Mother Tree.

As an architect-in-training, I studied the Tree of Life from authors such as Roger Cook, Margaret Barker, and Mircea Eliade. As a new mother continuing her poetic quest, I was led to an even deeper personal engagement with this sacred symbol. In the wilderness of my separateness from any other experience I'd known, I thirsted for other women, for a space to speak the unspeakable about our bodies, about the symbols in our limbs and hearts.

The Tree of Life has for millennia been a symbol of the Divine Mother. In the Old Testament, the tree is the representation of Asherah, the Great Mother to the ancient Israelites. She represents eternal life in the most primal sense, as the preserver of the interrelationships of all beings and the Earth around them.

Abraham's earliest form of temple worship was altered by King Josiah in the sixth century BCE to adhere with The Book of the Law, discovered during the temple's renovation. The worship reforms of supporters of this law code caused the loss of plain and precious things, including the older ideas, symbols, possibly entire rituals, and forms of words from the temple, including Asherah, Lady Wisdom. The removal of Asherah from the Holy of Holies of the temple was the removal of the urtext of women; the sacred script that unfolded their role in salvation, their unique language, their unique voice. It was the rejection of ecological wisdom, the mysteries of creation.

Having women in the built spaces and theological discourses of Mormonism is more than just a matter of equal representation; it is a matter of survival and salvation.

With our female Archetype absent from the discourse and relatively little language to describe Her, Mormon women are left with fewer resources than they need to traverse the terrain of their experience. I was left to answer the question: What does it mean as a woman to represent the Creatress, the natural world, in a time of ecological unraveling and with the silence of women just breaking?

The root of our ecological crisis lies in our separation from the Tree. Humankind's large-scale environmental degradations prove that the forces of industrialization perceive that natural systems' inherent value is inferior to extractable resources for immediate human consumption. The pride behind the wanton destruction of eternal networks in the physical and spiritual spheres of the wild is the same pride that removed the Divine Mother from Her temple throne, and attempts to accelerate the silencing of women.

The Tree at the Center is an eco-theological work that delves into the meaning of female exile and reveals that a new language is part of the way forward. Three instantiations of the Tree—the Tree of Ascent, the Tree of Fertility, and Asherah the Tree—all find expression in my contribution to the ancient but new vernacular for Mormon women. *The Tree at the Center* seeks to revive and revivify the Mormon people's relationship with nature and the wilderness Mother who is not separate from us. This is the story of women that has only been whispered peripherally in Mormonism. Women feel the presence of their exiled Mother, find Her encoded in the symbology of the temple and the wild earth, and are ready and waiting to participate in Her deciphering.

I.
THE TREE OF ASCENT

As soon as I reached God's unity, I became a bird, whose body was of Oneness and whose wings were of Everlastingness. I went on flying until I reached the expanse of eternity and in it I saw the Tree of Oneness.

> *—Abu Yazid Bastami, ninth-century Sufi poet*

NÜSHU*

*"Women's Script" of the rural villages of Jiangyong, China

Once there was a language
of women. Once
there was script for
"world" and "womb" outside
the characters of men.

Ticks of thread pulled
through cloth, belts, straps,
passwords embroidered
into the hems of women
who worshiped birds. Stories
passed from mother
to daughter, murmurations
of sky and land.

It is their motion I feel—strokes
laid like insect tracks,
bodies embracing—whipped air.
Virgules and arcs stalk my shadow,
unbearable as wings
that will never touch down.

It is all I can do not
to reach out and feel blindly
for the apparitions
of bird women, to shout, desperate
for tongues, *Teach me*
how to break open
my lips.

Once there was a clan
of sworn sisters. Once
they were feared.

HORIZON

I awoke to December washed
in pink diffusion, with
the softness of childhood
in my belly. As if

I were walking alone,
backlit in grasses
cut by a seemingly straight
path, the faint translucence of the inner
skin of an abalone shell hovering
between distant lines
of sky and land. And I felt

instinctually that there is also a voice, at this
distant opening in the sky
not of human kind, not of beast or rain,
that breaks my heart open
like Rilke's birds,

turning in chaotic weaves, scraping
for the updraft, for
the way out, and what is home
but my own heart sounding
itself against this
presence before me, against
itself—there the abalone—willing
the cosmos alive?

I don't know what it means
to finally reach the center of stillness—
this parted veil, the infinite longing
of the child's heart swallowed
in infinite light—what beginning
will be the end. Only

that the dirt is inseparable from my body,
my hand from the rustling heads,
my heart the beam of homecoming.

THE CENTER

When the time is right, the deep
nudging, that obscure shadow
will pull you in ways exact from sorrow
to longing for the ineffable landscape,
to that open field just over
the last horizon.

After the long journey
what you always hoped for—the deepest
cavern of mind with those treasures unnamed
and inescapable—resides here
at the central point of the clearing.

You know it: the axis of absolute reality.

It pulls and repels
as you circle—dusk to dawn—
until you understand its many iterations:
a pillar of light, a totem of ancestors,
a tree forever ascending.

When you stop orbiting
(if you ever do) do you
approach the deep humming
or do you retreat?

If you climb to the top and partake of its fruit
are you consumed? Turned
into something else altogether,
the alchemy complete?

Is our journey here, after all,
to return us to the navel we left,
plant our souls in the center and become
another center?

Interchanging auditorium
and stage
in the cosmic odeum of beholding
and being beheld?

And finally you must discern
the robed figure beside you
in the periphery of stars, whose stirrings
you take on as your own.

FALLACY OF A DISTANT SKY GOD

The Gods said

Let our bodies
plummet
in showers
and bend
as finely bladed
grass.

Let us place
our eyes
with mirth
in the dew.

And under
every bridge,

a thin space,

full of dark
sudden wings,
white feathered
heads,

breaking cloudless
skies with
enough awe
to fissure the
world.

THE TREE OF LIFE

1 Nephi 11:9-23
2 Enoch 22

Lehi lifts his gaze to the end
of the path, seeing more
than he could imagine:
exiled Asherah

illuminates his way, expands
into every corner of the universe, into
fractals upon fractals of branches—
love multiplying
outside of time.

There, on the vast field
numberless paths
gather creation, converge at Her trunk
—cheetah and aspen
taste the fiery white fruit.

Her song is the sacred script
of flowers, equations of stars and tissue.

Here, he writes, *there is
no salvation without
the salmon and the yew.*

His feet transfigure at Her roots.
Temporary seraph, he feels earth
about to flame. And then a voice, rolling:

*Brush his skin with my delightful oil,
and clothe him in my glory, greater
than the greatest light.*

Above his head women and men
ascend the morning dew.

11

WORLD TREE

In the beginning I was
seed concealed in loam,
swelling for a beam of light
to extend my white neck—a flick,
a sprout—into a leafy head.

From sapling springs
my fathomless boughs into Thor's Oak.

At the seam of unassailable
obscurity, the most tender blues
finger through my branches.
Below Jerusalem's coral clouds,
I blossom over the four
cardinal rivers, bare
twelve manner of fruits—

Buddha's sacred bodhi, I brace
him against the demon Mara
until he climbs into my arms, beyond
terrestrial desire.

I am poured and beaten gold,
the seven-branched menorah
of Moses' tabernacle.

I am the kadamba tree
where Krishna sustains
the life of the universe with song,
drawing the hearts of all beings
towards my trunk.

The myrrh tree, I birth Adonis
from my fissured side. As Isis,
I suckle Thoutmosis III
in the guise of a sycamore.

I am the Maypole, the corn stalk,
roots weaving the underworld.

The holy feet descending
the rungs of Jacob's dreams.

Moses 7:53

THE CALL

All my foliage, in heaps—
golds, crimson, all the sweet
oranges—a pyre of parting
and light.

As my fruit ripens in heat
and rain, seasons pass through
root and heart. How my changeless trunk
meets my change-full boughs—
an imitation

of the spinning cosmos: forever
moving, forever still. In me
all things came to be—the honey,
the sting—my body—your body ultimately
replaced, effecting the cure.

We plunge deep
into mythical time, to firmaments parting,
to the first dragonfly wing etched, then
humming. *Let there be*, I said,
and there was.

Immutable center,
broad as eternity—who shall climb
up by me and come forth—endless
blooming—
into the breadth of eternity, with songs
of everlasting joy?

HOLY OF HOLIES
2 Enoch 23:1

After the final ascent,
Enoch's eyes open
on the womb of Solomon's temple—
a cube of fire, an aperture into the throngs—
all those dancing figures.

Did you think the godly mysteries
would be bodies thrumming to the canon
of creation? I want to know

what it means to pull light from dark,
how we were woven before
sun and moon bore sway over tides
and land—

what is written on the fleshy walls
of my womb. Show me in what
perfect script atoms say yes
and atoms say no to formulas unseen
yet recited over and over until
the universe is one swelling requiem.

II.
THE TREE OF FERTILITY

All religious experiences connected with
fecundity and birth have a cosmic structure.
The sacrality of woman depends on
the holiness of the earth.

–Mircea Eliade

They shall not hurt nor destroy in all my
holy mountain: for the earth shall be full
of the knowledge of the Lord,
as the waters cover the sea.

–Isaiah 11:9

SALVATION PANTOUM

Before the beginning, the dragonfly
peels its inky wings off the pages of the gods
who know how it will catch its prey in flight,
how its ancestors will form its name.

Its inky wings peel off the pages of the gods
revealing its iridescence and love of water,
how its ancestors will form its name and
frame its ties to midge and moth, to countless others.

Its iridescence and love of water
hedge the earth from destruction. *How*, you say,
*is connection to countless others
a promise of not only survival but salvation?*

They hedge the earth from destruction. *How?* you say.
Through fulfillment of the measure of their creation,
a promise of not only survival but salvation—
the lion and the lamb, forever on the earth.

Through fulfillment of the measure of their creation
—the ant, the bear, the maple exalted—
the lion and the lamb will live forever on the earth,
their names written in the Book of Life.

The ant, the bear, the maple exalted,
sing songs of everlasting joy—eye to eye—
their names written in the Book of Life
before the first oceans, with the dragonfly.

FROM EVE'S IMPERATIVE GUIDE ON HOW TO TEND AND TILL THE EARTH OUR MOTHER: HOW TO CONDUCT A PRESCRIBED BURN IN GRASSLAND

First, you must know that the moment
you decide to unfurl the fires
determines the plants which will
be benefited and controlled, the impact
on wildlife, how safely
you will burn.

A fire in late spring will rein in the woody
vegetation and cool season grasses, but
will not benefit the wildflowers. The soil
surface should be damp. Nesting times
should always be checked.

The best time for spring fires
is late March into April, morning
or evening when the relative
humidity and temperature
are not changing as rapidly as
during the daylight hours.

The drier the area the earlier the burn
should be to avoid damaging the earliest blooming
wildflowers. Relative humidity between fifty
and seventy percent is best. Below
fifty grasses will spark
very hot fires. Above seventy
the fire finds it hard to catch.

The wind should be between three
and seven miles per hour, remaining steady.

And you must consider the burn techniques:
back fire, parallel fire, perimeter fire, and strip head fire.
Tools to ignite, tools to control, safety equipment.

When choosing a burn technique, remember
your level of experience,
and that of your burn crew.

Notify the neighbors.

FULL CIRCLE

Her response is a bark beetle
the size of a matchstick tip, disappearing
on the trunk of a great and ailing pine.

The skittering, skeletal legs who, en masse,
are more devastating than a hurricane
with their honed sensitivity to wind change,
sniffing out vulnerabilities in the flesh—

avail themselves of meat that will feed
generations as they bite, piranha-style,
through acre on acre of wood.

Some have crossed oceans to find harvest
in this new world, prey defenseless to their
particular brand of torture and execution. Others,

evolved with the invaded, muscle
new weapons more cutting than the last, find
the exhaustion of fragmented forests
delicious.

This is the natural way—armies devouring
into gluttonous stupors, pushing
toward the edge of everything.

Mother sits at both heads of the feasting table
performing the work of salvation:
the tree, the beetle.

REPRISE

Who, if I cried out, would hear
on the edge of this shrinking sphere?

Bird, jaguar and moon—
woman in flight, stalk and song.

On the border of this inner land
I stand—rainforest trapped
by clear-cut line, the cacophony
of insect and scarlet macaw
devastated. Spiders and frogs,
unnamed creatures of dusk and dawn,
rise like prayers
from baked, red mud.

Man, there once was
rapture in the arms
of what you don't understand.

What is left
to be dislodged,
reinterpreted will not
always be
the stream, the mountain,
the flying fox and its durian tree;
there is no help
in a wingless sky.

THE EVER EXISTENT IMAGE

> The Oak dies as well as the Lettuce, but its Eternal Image & Individuality never dies but returns by its seed; just so the Imaginative Image returns by the seed of Contemplative Thought.
>
> –William Blake

It's not until December
that I notice the hunched spirits
in my backyard, begging not
to be released. Body

husks, shriveled
fingers, clutching rusted
mesh towers. Ghost tomatoes
refuse departure from their place
of birth, citing endless regeneration
in bone-white seeds.

Pulling at their roots
provokes a surprising shot
of sympathy
pain down
my body, the resistance
as real as my child's legs wrapped
around my waist
at bedtime. The light

of inner necessity
is still springing—stems of
ever-blooming fragrance, yellow hips
full of a "how blue" sky.

My son still believes in
their summer-sweet savor,
points and says "num," points
and sees.

BABA YAGA

She lowers her haunches
onto the chair in front of me, heaving.
Two yellow eyes and a snarl—
there is nowhere else.

Full-throated and roving now,
she is the smell of good mud,
all the crowning heads, my sagging
breasts.

The howl!—she springs
into my chest, deep into my gut, tongue
wagging, *You knew I would come.*

It is too late to struggle, she has me
by the heart—bony fingers exacting
surrender to a four-chambered song
of what should live and what should die.

Perched on the rim of my lungs
she listens—oh, how she raises
my anxious desiccation to the sea,
infuses my blood with the secrets
of birds.

She pokes my grasses
through the snow, works invention
where language is made—

bids the wild lands
behind my eyes
Come on.

WOMAN OF WILLENDORF

After your heavy breasts,
the black navel, the thresh
of thighs over doughy knees,
an arc of shadow plays
above a descending slit
into that eternal chamber
of love and war.

Tight knees will not hide
the fabric of the veil—pleasure
and pain in the fragments of red ochre
pigment tucked in your crevasses, as if
to say, *here is where it matters at all*—life

red as the earth, as wine, as
the flecks of blood all over my son's
emergent body on my hollow belly.

Because you look more like a portal
than a woman with a name, rings
of gases and meteors shroud your lofty summit—
plaits of planetary vision.

Your stacked spheres heave
until you can no longer stand—
head and legs undoing counterbalance
to mounting buttocks
and that begotten belly.

A talisman of women-talk,
the dazzler, the dark, you eat pieces
of the All and from the deep mine
of our own bellies, we
are the goddesses
of the obscene.

TREASURES IN HEAVEN

A whale, a moon,
a boat ready
to expose
the belly of each,
rock me, hip

to hip. Shake
the frame, fist.
Unclench.
Show me
the dark,
wet
head.

LABOR

When the body
fills with tiny hooves
pressing in the early hours
before dawn (some

prodding softest flowers)
reverberations
of past lives cities open doors

mourn the already
granulated shadows
of a new dawn—Christmas crowning—
the first news of chains
broken

(Flanks flash white celestial blue
primordial waves press
my womb)

the way out they say is through
never breaching
the cold earth the kingdom never
over the next horizon

We clan of mothers remember
the light parted the shells dashed the
pearl
drawn out
from still-clattering chambers
of the deepest sweetest
twists of tissue There

is the Mother on bended knee
in the great mind of the body
spurring the horses on
and on and on

"PLATE 18," BY UNKNOWN

I am staring at "Plate 18"—pink fire
crowns a solid blue oval, a mask
floating without eyes,
a void dressed
by magenta moss.

A password finally spoken
would look like this,
the moment when the hero lifts
her eyes, fear and awe
in her throat
as the veil lifts. It sounds

in the stretching of the fetus
in my side—the slow
deliberate push
that causes the tides
in my body to
sing a new song.

I breathe out a child
from the churning whirlpool
of my womb, a song suspended
in magenta clouds—
a pulsing navy *Om*
rings out
between my legs—

the gong that begins
and ends divine appearing.

A blue thumb
presses my placenta out, the Tree
of Life framed in the brightest day.

And maybe,
actually and finally, it is
the embodiment
of my body—a portal between
branches steeped in celestial light
and the roots of the underworld—

the long receiving
of the beginning
and end.

"Plate 18," by Unknown.

From *Tantra Song*, selected & with writings by Franck André Jamme.

AS A MOTHER

I lie on my side
in the cool of our maple.
Your small body balances
against the curve of my hip.
I speak to you and hear
myself as if from across a room—
a phenomenon of postpartum.

I never desired to be a symbol,
but since the Feminine Divine
brought up your soft round
warmth from my depths
crawling on my chest to coo and sigh, I
am one working prism of Her endless
blinking body.

My voice is your sacred pole
holding up the sky.

It rises from my frame, leaving
Earth, to collapse
space and time—and returns here
to the grass, to
the soft pink
of dusk.

The Mother's *Om*
moves around your twists of bone
and muscle, then further
back to the shadowy
chambers of deeper knowing
each smaller than the one before, spiraling
toward the final and the first—
the holy of holies.

I never asked to be the center,
the eternal tree,
a venus belly,
etched. But as your sweet body
latches to my breast, I
am Eve, the sun of my son—
who will carry the tree through himself
when he multiplies
and replenishes the earth.

NINE MONTHS POSTPARTUM

You don't remember, so I tell you
under the maple
how I was the bridge
that landed you safely
under a full summer moon.
I was the parted veil.

I tell you also, though not in words,
how I have never
felt so disconnected
from the earth
and the heavens
that I breached
—from the dirt, from the I Am—thunder
not in sound but in force
used to move up my legs,
vibrations grounding
me here, the light above
grounding me there.

I wanted to be
the constant revolving sun
for you, son
dropped like an arrow,
but instead I am
the molted skin of an unclaimed
creature—full dust and wind—
trying to understand
how everything left me
when I had you.

How, with your shimmering
small life, I mostly think about death, how
suns do burn out, how
this gorgeous spreading maple
will one day succumb
to a break in its bark, and give way
to spores, then beetles,
then woodpecker. Emerald
mosses instead of wood.

I tell you, I think it's okay to mourn
the loss of things we cannot name,
as what tethered me
became shadow, as the infant you
rolled down my back,
your grey beard waving.

POSTPARTUM DEPRESSION

In a tired rising up of something
that resembled longing, a clap

of smoke surfacing spirits
of my denouement—the world
not nothing, but
slumbering deeper
than ever before—

not even the smell
of his honey milk skin,
the sweetest warmth
my body will ever feel, not
his small cry forming
my deepest heart,
could make feet touch
ground, could rally a life
now posthumanus.

To "see things as they really are"
was a mirror without a face
left hovering in the void
growing each time no one
could tell me from where
the imbalance came, why
the dirty dishes in the sink robbed me
of self, gutted me like the last
salmon still swimming
against the current, swimming with

all the fervor and heat of a thing
that must continue
through its seed, must
meet its natural end, only

to be plucked out
by a clawed hand, another
deep hunger that must
be satisfied.

Or like those eclipsing the river
only to crash body on
body on rock, dashing themselves
in shiny strips.

WOMAN LIKE A WOLF

There are three conditions
in which wolves kill excessively.
With rabies or distemper,

or when the rhythm of cyclic knowing
halts its massive cogs, extending
a winter's reign that strands deer and wolf alike
in mounding snowfall.

When thaw finally breaks famine,
the deer, the hyperbolic treasure
exalted in the wolves' memory, flee
for the next life while the pursuing pack
splits the forest in a blinding sheen,
pouring teeth into the deers' frenzied flanks.

Light spills into their bellies. The alpha
female bares fangs at her cubs.
Into blossoming pink snow, possession's
immeasurable consequence. Crimson drops
glisten down their legs,
springloaded.

PALIMPSEST

My pelvis sat next to me
on my couch, the way
strangers do, turned
toward me with that attentive
politeness that borders
on intrusion.

If you believe me, then
I asked for her name
and she became Wolf, bent low.
Her mournful eyes shifted

and we stood in familiar woods—
thin pines, a bank of snow,
drifting. She rocked her lean
body, right
left
and ran.

And then I knew
her as Solitude, so I followed
deep into the land that had
birthed my only child.

Would you believe me
if I told you that Wildness
is also a name for Pelvis,
Wolf, who is Solitude
all written
on the walls
of my womb, a palimpsest—
scripted, washed,
scripted—with the ordinances
of creation?

If you believe me, then
Sorrow is our common name.

MISCARRIAGE

The crabapple above is brittle-black.
Skirting branches feel the lulling
breath beyond winter, muster a double display
of red fruit. Only in this moment

does life mean all the seeds left, arrayed
as sweetest passing. What lasts
when you can no longer feel
the snow or scrub jay interrupting the deep
meditation of your boughs?

Job 32:8; 33:4

CREATION

Shaddai,
clothed with the sun,
hovers over the face
of the waters, belly

surging.

The sea surrounding
Her heavenly throne,

separates

bounding the firmament below—
releasing forms into flesh—
an arching whale,
foal in sac,
a camel, crying.

Below Her closing eyes
a horse is baptized in foam.
Into the land of passing
shadows, he walks the line
into the first hood of dusk.

Now at rest, like the small rustle
of fruit falling, the blackened
nostrils free of the waves, flare.
It seems there is no turning back.

RENASCENCE

I birth my own body,
unspool,
hand back the rib.

I dream of woman-made
woman, of which
man-made woman cannot conceive.
I birth my own

name from the end of a cord
still pulsing under
eternal, multifloras boughs,
break sac, emerge,
effulgent and ravenous
for a mother-tongue and a mother-land—

Next to me a lion and a lamb
purr in the grass. Every forest is green
and rising,
rising.

III.
ASHERAH THE TREE

Isaiah linked the desolation of the land
to the loss of the Lady,
and it is likely that he saw the restoration
of creation as Her return.

—Margaret Barker

Gaze on the *raz nihyeh* (the mystery of becoming)
and know the paths of everything that lives.

—Qumran Texts

ONE THOUSAND TWO HUNDRED SIXTY DAYS

Revelation 12:6-14

Sometimes in a long white
gown, often in tattered brown
wool, always with two wings
of a great eagle on Her back, Asherah
circles the edges
of the square, of the wilderness where
we have left Her,
watching.

Sometimes in the towering sphere
of the temple we continue to build,
the void at its center, the scar
of Her uprooting
flickers Her image—white
bark and meat, branch and trunk,
the softness of Her belly fruit—plump
pears, pomegranates—
pulling on the softness
of my womb.

THE TREE AT THE CENTER

We talk often
of the Son's surrender
His long suffering, His forever
atoning—the shards
of the universe, gathered
to reconcile all
the ways in which God
has been lost
to us.

I want to know
about the surrender
of the Mother, if it felt at all
like a body
laid flat
as creation writhed
shaking the bed
of Earth while Her mind
broke
into shards, into the wilderness
into the wolf. No word, no language
separate from the surging
womb.

I want to know
how death hit Her square
on the meatiest turn
of Her trunk, then dragged Her
from the forest—the embroidered branches
rent from Solomon's temple—
to pierce Her stiff arms
with Her son's.

I want to know
how a forest survives
without trees, how
we will welcome the Son
with the fires
still burning.

PARTICLE MOTHER

It is hard
to find you
dismantled
down to atoms
by generations of men
who dragged you
by the hair
from the temple, who

burned your limbs
at every shrine, leaving less
than an adumbration
in the chronicles
of a people longing
for religion.

A shadow would at least
give rhythm
to your gait,
prowl or shift,
a manifestation of how wind
might part for you.

What corners
you keep.

Should you waver
between absence
and arrival, I could at least
draw in
your elusive fragrance
and remember
your passing cloud—
possess some assurance
of heat
and response.

Sometimes in the wave
of the pines, in
a stillness that dilates
my mind into dissolution,

I feel you
everywhere
next to me,
shadowing my shadow,
humming incantations
that parted the water
over the land.

The Gospel of Philip
Job 38:33-36

THE OLDER COVENANT

Take me back
before the broken tablets,
back to the secrets of winds
unfurled, constellations rising
in a new horizon, mud
and branch called by name.

I know of the Tree, good
and evil swirling
in its fruit, alive
before the lesser law
became our golden calf.

Lady Wisdom wanders,
knows too well
that nothing transgresses
its appointed order
but we.

Take me back
to the pattern of the heavens
sewn into the lining
of Her dress.

Give me the wisdom
of the ant, she who
needs no instruction
on how to gather
and harvest, on the true
measure of her
creation.

Grant me a gaze
into the Holy
of Holies that I may know
the paths of everything
that lives.

CUBE OF FIRE*

And maybe we have to consider
that if we find the fluttering heat
of maternal wings missing,
the cube of fire, the heart of creation now
a place of darkness, where

love outside time and every dancing figure
of Ezekiel's Living Ones
have passed,

that She, once in the midst of everything,
like the subtlest, sweetest fragrance of home,
must be restored. And who

are these temple priests
slated to return—the shadow of exile
dusting their trailing robes,
palm leaves in hand—if not you,
if not me?

*The Cube of Fire, a 20-cubit cube lined with gold, was the Holy of Holies in the Jerusalem temple and the residence of the Mother of the Lord (1 Kings 6:20). It represented the origin and heart of creation.

THE MERCY SEAT

Moses 7:48

Enoch stands on the eternal mount,
turning pages of land and sea
from the Hadean
through ages rising with stone,
falling with sword.

From her bowels—the seat
of tenderness—he hears the earth
lamenting her children.

I can't know if it was my generation
who made her finally cry out, *How long?*

She waits to be cleansed from webs
of greedy tongues, rivers and rivers of blood
for a season of righteousness before all
becomes present
before her.

Eclipsing every day like the unsettling song
of the mourning dove, like
a land I once loved now elusive—
is this: sorrow is the heart of mercy, never
to depart. Not before the lion and the lamb,
not after.

Ezekiel 34
Odes of Solomon
11:14-15; 36:6

EZEKIEL'S VISIONS

I.

He sees Her leave from the north gate
to the threshold of the temple, the inner
court filling with the Cloud,
with brightness as She passed. Through
the city, dust covers Her train.

A river of white sashes follow, murmuring
incantations over cupped hands full
of incense, to the east mountain—
the savor of Her exile.

II.

On the Day of Atonement
Her return is as Her departure,
". . . the sound of many waters."

A rush of angels and measuring reeds, laws
poured out in a clamor of tongues, framing
cubit by cubit.

To the Holy of Holies, through the eastern gate,
Glory fills the temple—a river springs
from its center, Her branches spreading
on its banks, whose leaves
are for healing.

III.

Whose fruit is for wisdom and whose oil
is for anointing, to open the eyes to unerring
knowledge of what exists. She, the bond who holds
all things in harmony, She, the seal of creation, pours
out of the mouth of the Most High,
covering the earth like a mist.

IV.

My eyes were enlightened and my face
received the dew.

Genesis 1:27
Job 28:23-24

SHE WHO JOINS TOGETHER

Since the cloven fruit,
whose name we can't remember,
since Adam pulled themselves apart,

the world separates.

The longest thread of life in me
knows it can't remember the passwords
once spoken, that held our place
with the stars, only

that the seal of creation is Her name, finally spoken—
the return of forest, the Amen reembodied,
visions of eternal forms
Abraham saw on nights thick
with stars—of which we know nothing.

There, is Wisdom,
in the order, traces,
and nerves, new names
to bind us—clan of lions—more pure
than our eyes at birth.

WO, WO IS ME, THE MOTHER OF MEN

Moses 7:48

In my sky
there is a dove, heart
pumping hot
as a sun.

When she rests on my singular
branches, when
she buries her pebble skull
under smoke wings,

the subtle pressure
stirs my leaves. Trunk
and roots
expand with joy
gone out of me—

righteousness abiding on my face.

SALVATION

What if it is you, this whole time,
under the Oak of Moreh,
yes, you, hungering as Abraham,
for the faces of the Gods,
to be sealed up
to the ancestors—to greatest grandfather,
daughters of Eve, to forest, to wolf.

There, under that ancient tree,
staring into Shaddai's flaming tongues,
you must ask for what you really want.

Because this isn't just a tale
of heirophony, but your own life,
you must plead as desperately as the Father
of our Fathers for the Cloud of Glory
to swallow you up. Say:

Oh Shaddai! Save me in your fruitful boughs,
make it sure that I partake
and am consumed by your eyes,
healed from my wandering heart.

IN ONE

He commends His soul to be ferried
across the listening waters
of the underworld.

White pears of the endless night
offer themselves along His path
as spirits with countless divisions of mind
press in on all sides.

Mother shows Him how to dive
into soul after soul, body blending
until separation and sorrow ad infinitum

break Him. Every spirit's past and present
transposes self, pleading to be infinitely known
in order to exist infinitely.

Carrying even my womb, He expands me out of time.

Below all things and through
all things He bears the possessed
out of the black waters, weaves a new wisdom
that shudders the earth.

THE GROVE

Joseph enters. A beetle
weaves a shock of orange
through early decay. Dogwood
and wild rose rouse
under beech and elm.

A collective sigh
waves the canopy above,
dilating the distant blue.

From his lips
—a cry—

Mother, Her thousand ears,
Her thousand eyes, Her fragrance
suffusing, opens the heavens
upon Her son—pillar descending—

held to Her chest, flat on his back
in the seat of the Throne, in

Her thousand branches adorning the long climb
into the milky stars—legs gripping
the murky underworld—

hosts and hosts and hosts and hosts.

ACKNOWLEDGMENTS

The author thanks the editors of the following publications in which these poems first appeared:

Dialogue: A Journal of Mormon Thought: "One Thousand Two Hundred Sixty Days," "The Tree at the Center," and "The Older Covenant"
Exponent II: "Nine Months Postpartum"
Psaltery & Lyre: "Nüshu," "Labor"
Segullah: "The Grove" (Segullah 2019 Poetry Contest "If You Only Knew"; 2nd place award)
Young Ravens Literary Review: "As a Mother"

NOTES

"HORIZON" Inspired by "Ah, not to be cut off" by Rainer Maria Rilke.

"THE TREE OF LIFE" In Lehi's and Nephi's visions of the tree of life they see the tree, a river of filthy water (though Lehi didn't notice the filthiness), and a building on the opposite bank that was high and lifted up, which collapsed spectacularly. This maps directly onto the geography of Jerusalem, particularly at the time of Christ (with the giant temple platform on impossibly high walls when viewed from the Kidron Valley).

The Garden of Gethsemane, a sacred grove, sits on the slope of the hill facing the temple. Margaret Barker suggests that Ezekiel's vision in Ezekiel 10 was a vision of the Divine Mother leaving the temple moving eastward across the threshold of the temple, an echo of the woman driven into the wilderness from Revelation 12. If She were a tree—one of Her symbols that was purged from the temple in Ezekiel/Lehi's day—that tree would come to rest in the wilderness east of the temple, perhaps symbolically on the Mount of Olives.

The river of water next to the Mount of Olives is the Kidron River. It runs through a valley of tombs, and was where Hezekiah's priests took the unclean items from the inner chambers of the temple to cleanse the temple (2 Chr. 29:16 NRSV).

The temple, particularly at the time of Christ, was a den of thieves, the headquarters of those who mocked and slew Christ and his followers. Its giant stones were pulled down in 70 CE.

The second set of italicized lines in the poem comes from one translation of 2 Enoch 22:

> And The Lord said to Michael, "Go, and extract Enoch from his earthly clothing. Anoint him with My delightful oil, and put him into the clothes of My Glory." So Michael did, just as The Lord said to him. He anointed me and he clothed me. The appearance of that oil is greater than the greatest light, and its ointment is like sweet dew, and its fragrance myrrh; it is like the rays of the glittering sun.
>
> I looked at myself and I had become like one of his glorious ones, and there was no observable difference.

"HOLY OF HOLIES" 2 Enoch 23:1: "And he was telling me all the works of heaven, earth and sea, and all the elements, their passages and goings, and the thunderings of the thunders, the sun and moon, the goings and changes of the stars, the seasons, years, days, and hours, the risings of the wind, the numbers of the angels, and the formation of their songs, and all human things, the tongue of every human song and life, the commandments, instructions, and sweet-voiced singings, and all things that it is fitting to learn."

"FROM EVE'S IMPERATIVE GUIDE ON HOW TO TEND AND TILL THE EARTH OUR MOTHER: HOW TO CONDUCT A PRESCRIBED BURN IN GRASSLAND" Instructions adapted from: Sargent, M.S and Carter, K.S., ed. 1999. *Managing Michigan Wildlife: A Landowners Guide*. Michigan United Conservation Clubs, East Lansing, MI.

"REPRISE" Inspired by "First Elegy" from *Duino Elegies*, by Rainer Maria Rilke.

"BABA YAGA" Baba Yaga represents the "Wild Woman" (the intuition of a woman's psyche) in the aspect of a witch. Like the word *wild*, the word *witch* is now understood as a pejorative, but used to be a title given to women healers. The word *witch* derives from the word *wit*, meaning wise.

The line, "works invention where language is made," taken from *Women Who Run with the Wolves: Myths and Stories of the Wild Woman Archetype*, by Clarissa Pinkola Estés, 1996.

The literal translation of *raz nihyeh* is "the secret of the ways things are," given by Margaret Barker in her book, *The Mother of the Lord Volume I: The Lady in the Temple*, p.107.

"SHE WHO JOINS TOGETHER" The name "Adam" refers to Adam and Eve, as in Genesis 5:2: "Male and female created he them; and blessed them, and called their name Adam, in the day when they were created."

"SALVATION" Abram erected the first altar at Shechem under a tree called the Oak of Moreh, because the Lord appeared to him there (Gen. 12:4-7). Moreh means "teacher," which suggests that it was a significant tree. In Hebrew script, the word Moreh is very similar to Shaddai, an ancient title for Mother and the name of the God of the patriarchs (Exod. 6:3).

KATHRYN KNIGHT SONNTAG is a landscape designer and land planner in Salt Lake City. She has a BA in English, a BS in environmental studies and a master's in landscape architecture and environmental planning. Her poems and essays have appeared in many publications, including: *Shades: The University of Utah's Literary Magazine*; *Wilderness Interface Zone*; *Young Ravens Literary Review*; *Exponent II*; *Psaltery & Lyre*; *Segullah*; and *Dialogue: A Journal of Mormon Thought*. She loves to hike with her husband and son.

kathrynknightsonntag.com

www.ingramcontent.com/pod-product-compliance
Lightning Source LLC
Chambersburg PA
CBHW022014120526
44592CB00034B/810